SEE GOD
Today

TRILOGY

PROFESSIONAL PUBLISHING MEETS POWERFUL PROMOTION

A wholly owned subsidiary of **TBN**

...ion about special discounts for bulk purchases, please contact Trilogy Christian

...in the United States of America

...3 2 1

...gress Cataloging-in-Publication Data is available.

...088-207-2

...088-208-9 (ebook)

SEE GOD
Today

A Gratitude Journal For Tho...

LINDA FAR...

Copyr...

All Sc...
INTER...
Used by...

Scriptur...
Edition:...

All rights...
whatsoever...
Michelle...

Trilogy Ch...
Network.

For informa...
Publishing.

Manufactured...

10 9 8 7 6 5 4...

Library of Con...

ISBN 978-1-64...

ISBN 978-1-64...

Dedication

This journal is dedicated to my beautiful daughter, Assata, for reminding me of the healing grace and restorative power of gratitude.

and

To my surgeon, Dr. Dawn Leonard, for her attentive care, tender kindness and unfailing encouragement.

Foreword

For more than twenty years, I have wondered when and how my friend and sister in Christ, Linda Lewis, would find the time and energy to share her remarkable story of how she managed life.

As a committed mother, accomplished professional and devout Christian, she battled and survived the trials and trauma associated with cancer.

Along with many, I remain amazed by how she has been able to demonstrate grace, courage, stamina and unyielding faith through such difficult and trying times.

Her heroic story of resiliency and unrelenting faith will without a doubt, encourage others who may be facing life's hard trials.

—Rev. David W. Young

"The light of the body is the eye:
If therefore thine eye be single,
Thy whole body shall be full of light."
— MATTHEW 6:22 (KJV)

Cancer

"Cannot take away your faith,
Shatter your hope or lessen your love.

It cannot destroy true friendships,
Invade your soul or take away eternal life.

It cannot conquer your spirit or invalidate
Your essential meaning."
— UNKNOWN

Introduction

It is truly amazing how much we take things for granted while on this journey of life without seriously giving thought about what we say and how we respond. Very often, we only pause to think about or appreciate how fortunate we are after something catastrophic happens.

Fortunately, I had the privilege and presence of mind during my only daughter's formative years to communicate with her in a manner which would, years later, produce a subtle but phenomenal impact upon my life. At that time, my intention was to create an awareness of the presence of God in her life in spite of challenging or difficult circumstances.

However, little did I know that our line of communication and the seeds that I had sown during that process would bear tremendous fruit later in my personal life. No one could have told me that this would have impacted me in such a miraculous way and sustain me at the lowest level of my life when I was diagnosed with breast cancer.

See God Today is a gratitude journal for persons who have been impacted by cancer. It is intended to serve as a resourceful instrument to bring comfort and a level of joy during very trying times for anyone who is battling cancer. It was created to inspire and motivate us to look beyond our immediate concerns or worries and by faith, search to *"See God"* in order to recapture hope, happiness and moments of peace.

The journal entries are intended to invite you to appreciate your present blessings which so often, lie unrecognized in our lives. More importantly, this journal seeks to promote introspection and foster healing. The passages will facilitate the beauty of grace, healing and strength. They will also remarkably enhance the quality of everyday life!

The expression, *"Seeing God"* is an awakening. It is also an acknowledgment and celebration of the existing (right now) benefits and gifts from God; even while at the core of our encounters with cancer, such an unwelcomed and life-threatening disease.

As a cancer survivor, I have learned to better appreciate the experience of chronicling God's grace, goodness and mercy through journaling. I encourage you to maximize this opportunity and reflect upon these verses designed exclusively for your inspiration and holistic healing.

You will recognize that God never leaves us. He is able and he is always present to comfort and heal our emotional and physical wounds. Use this journal as a daily practice. Read one entry and write a contemplation each day. My prayer is that this experience of gratitude will minister to your life. Be blessed and be healed!

Contents

JOURNALING 1

Gratitude

"Blessed are the pure in heart for they shall see God."
— *MATTHEW 5:8 (KJV)*

Gratitude

"Gratitude can turn denial into acceptance, chaos into order, and confusion into clarity. It can turn a meal into a feast, a house into a home, a stranger into a friend." [1]

Being thankful inspires me to consider that my situation may not be as bad as I think and, quite frankly, it could be worse. It causes me to notice that I have more than I may have realized. Life happens and without gratitude, we forget that God is still with us. A mindset of appreciation has the power to calm our fears and clear our vision so that we may be attentive to the many benefits that still remain present with us.

Embracing our gift of life with its many challenges helps to change our perspective and relax our bodies. We disempower thoughts entrenched in misfortune and distress as we redirect and recalibrate our energy toward gratitude. "Strong and happy thoughts build the body with vigor and grace." [2] Until and if we are able to, we will do and give more. We do not have to wait until tomorrow to be *"alright"*. We are *"alright"* already! So I will see my glass of life not as half empty but as having all that I need to quench my thirst with the hope of being filled with joy and abundance. I encourage you to:

"Bless the Lord....and forget not all of His benefits."
— PSALMS 103:2 (KJV)

---

[1] Melody Beattie, Author
[2] James Allen, As A Man Thinketh, pg. 11, 1903

Fourteen Benefits of Gratitude

1. Adds to Mental and Physical Health.

"*The benefits of expressing gratitude range from better physical health to improved mental alertness.*" Psychology Today, Susan Krauss Whitbourne, Ph.D; The Benefits of Gratitude, May 25, 2010. https://www.psychologytoday.com/us/blog/fulfillment-any-age/201005/giving-thanks-the-benefits-gratitude

2. Reduces Stress, Anxiety, and Depression.

"*Being thankful can help to relieve stress, depression and addictions, among other conditions.*"; Time.Com, Maia Szalavitz; Why Gratitude Isn't Just for Thanksgiving; Nov. 22, 2012. http://healthland.time.com/2012/11/22/why-gratitude-isnt-just-for-thanksgiving/

3. Changes the Mindset.

"*There exists scientific evidence and research that demonstrates the ability of gratitude to impact positive change to mood, motivation and mindset..*" How Gratitude Can Change Your Life, Catherine Robertson; 4/18/2017 https://www.patheos.com/blogs/justonething/2017/04/how-gratitude-can-change-your-life/

4. Raises Positive Chemicals in the Brain Which Help Heal

"*Gratitude can be a natural antidepressant. Certain neural circuits are activated. Production of dopamine and serotonin increases, and these neurotransmitters then travel neural pathways to the "bliss" center of the brain — similar to the mechanisms of many antidepressants. Practicing gratitude, therefore, can be a way to naturally create the same effects of medications and create feelings of contentment.*" The Neuroscience of Gratitude, Emily Fletcher, HuffPost; Life Blog, 11/24/2015. https://www.huffpost.com/entry/the-neuroscience-of-gratitude_b_8631392

5. Improves Sleep.

"Writing in a gratitude journal improves sleep." Forbes, Amy Morin, 7 Scientifically Proven Benefits of Gratitude That Will Motivate You To Give Thanks Years Round, 11-23-2014.
https://www.forbes.com/sites/amymorin/2014/11/23/7-scientifically-proven-benefits-of-gratitude-that-will-motivate-you-to-give-thanks-year-round/

6. Strengthens the Memory.

"Gratitude has been shown to contribute to well-being by boosting the retrieval of positive autobiographical memories. The benefit on memory was shown to promote successful closure of unpleasant open memories, ultimately contributing to happiness." Why Gratitude Enhances Well Being: What We Know, What We Need to Know; Robert A. Emmons and Anjali Mishra; August, 2010.
https://emmons.faculty.ucdavis.edu/wp-content/uploads/sites/90/2015/08/2011_2-16_Sheldon_Chapter-16-11.pdf

7. Increases Optimism.

"In a series of experiments, daily exercises, practices and listing of all the things you are thankful for, are linked with a brighter outlook on life and a greater sense of positivity."
Huffington Post, Life Wellness, 10 Reasons Why Gratitude is Healthy, November 22, 2012.
https://www.huffpost.com/entry/gratitude-healthy-benefits_n_2147182

8. Helps Build a Healthy Heart.

"Gratitude has been found to be associated with better mood, better sleep, less fatigue and lower levels of inflammatory biomarkers related to cardiac health, said Paul Mills, PhD, San Diego.
"A Grateful Heart is a Healthier Heart, American Psychological Association, April 9, 2015.
https://www.apa.org/news/press/releases/2015/04/grateful-heart.aspx

9. Restores Peace.

"Thankfulness creates gratitude which generates contentment that causes peace." Todd Stocker, Author
https://www.goodreads.com/quotes/936472-thankfulness-creates-gratitude-which-generates-contentment – that-causes-peace

10. Beautifies the Countenance.

"A happy heart makes the face cheerful." Proverbs 15:33 (NIV)
"You look so much better when you smile" Kurt Franklin, Songwriter, 2011

11. Revives Feelings of Happiness and Joy.

Professor of Psychology and Author, Sonja Lyubomirsky states that "people who are grateful are likely to be happier, hopeful and energetic, and they possess positive emotions more frequently." The Relationship Between Happiness and Gratitude, Lauren Suval; psychcentral.com/blog; August 2012.
https://psychcentral.com/blog/the-relationship-between-happiness-and-gratitude/

12. Boosts Self-esteem.

"Study participants who kept gratitude journals and practiced self-guided exercises slept better, exercised more, experienced increased positive emotions, progressed toward personal goals more quickly, and helped others more often." Living in Gratitude, Angeles Arrien,; A Journey That Will Change Your Life, pg. 10, Sounds True, Inc. Bouler, CO, 2011

13. Raises One's Frequency/Vibration.

"Every thought, word and action carries its own vibrational frequency and draws to it the same. The more positive your thoughts and words, the more positive your vibration. Gratitude raises your vibration as you count your blessings, allow yourself to experience a deep sense of thankfulness and keep a daily gratitude...." 12 Ways to Raise Your Vibration; Tanaaz, foreverconscious.com
https://foreverconscious.com/12-ways-to-raise-your-vibration

14. Improves Wellness.

A leading gratitude researcher, Robert A. Emmons, PhD, states that "in the face of serious trauma, adversity, and suffering, if people have a grateful disposition, they'll recover more quickly. I believe gratitude gives people a perspective from which they can interpret negative life events and help them guard against post-traumatic stress and lasting anxiety." Why Gratitude is Good, Robert Emmons, Greater Good Magazine, Science Based Insights for Meaningful Life, 11/16/2010. https://greatergood.berkeley.edu/article/item/why_gratitude_is_good

Obstacles That Can Inhibit Gratitude

"Pervasive negativity.
Having a strong sense of entitlement.
Traumatic life events (suffering).
Conflicting emotions."[3]

---

[3] Divya Hemnani, Train Your Brain to Look for the Good: The Science of Gratitude, Instrinsic Brilliance Institute, 9/4/2014

What It Means to "See God"

To see God is an act of faith. It is a belief that life still has meaning and beauty even in the midst of adverse circumstances and unpleasant situations that threaten hope and hinder peace.

It is an awareness of the uninterrupted presence of God.

It is taking time to appreciate each breath and acknowledge that there is so much to be thankful for.

It means to be daring enough to embrace a mindset that searches through hurdles of hurt, disappointment, and depression for the deep-rooted, ever-present light of joy.

It is trusting that one's inner light, when re-discovered and given permission, has power to emerge brilliantly through the darkest hours.

It is to recognize that love, hope and life will endure *in spite* of the winds of change and life's eventualities.

It is to know that we constantly have within our reach the tremendous ability and superior intelligence to glimpse through the denseness of fog and see beyond its stalling effect, those beautiful moments in life that have the audacity and invincibility *to survive* through it all.

My "See God Today" Experience

My expression to "See God Today" evolved from an experience that began many years ago when my daughter was in elementary school. I made a simple suggestion to her to "See God" during the course of her day. I had no idea that those words would return to visit me years later to make an indelible impact that changed the trajectory of my emotions when I suffered and went through the unforeseen storm of cancer.

Going through this distressful time with the declaration to "See God Today" caused a radical transformation from a preoccupation with fear and self-pity, to a posture of hope and a greater appreciation for life. I had not deeply realized the inherent effect of those three words until that assertion caused me to experience an authentic and deep shift within.

My story began when this creative declaration was complemented with a kiss as I said goodbye to my daughter as she went on her way to school. That daily affirmation was intended to inspire and empower her, as well as offer a positive and cheerful perspective to an upcoming young mind that was still open to believe.

As an adult, I knew that life would bring rainy days but I wanted her to be carefree, happy and equipped with a way of thinking that could help her to quickly overcome worry and negativity. Therefore, I would happily urge her to "See God Today!" Nonetheless, there were times when we would talk about certain unavoidable challenges and after our conversations, I would ask "Did you see God today?" Amazingly, she began to ponder and tell me of experiences that made her smile during the day.

As she reflected, she would recall moments such as, "I found a dollar; my teacher said I did well in class; or I made a new friend!" It gave her an opportunity to remember the highlights and good things she had encountered during the course of her daily activities. This shift in her thinking to an attitude of gratitude, brought about a sense of contentment and caused her to experience happiness and joy.

As time passed on and for no apparent reason, we stopped sharing our *"See God Today"* experiences and it eventually escaped my memory.

Many years later while I was at work, a co-worker came into my office and sadly informed me that a lump was found in her breast. As we looked deeply into each other's eyes, I felt her fear and distress. We shared words of love and encouragement and later, she fortunately discovered that she did not have cancer. However, her experience reminded me that I had not gone for my regular mammogram appointment so I was compelled to call and schedule my annual exam.

Because my mammogram was a routine visit, I was not worried. But to my surprise and after going through several tests, I was later diagnosed with breast cancer. I did not initially respond in the strength and composure as many others. I was floored! Who? Me? I eat healthy! I can't believe it! I prayed. I cried. Yes...I was grieved.

As I searched for understanding, I learned that my "why me" reaction did not empower me. It only led me to feelings of defeat, hurt and betrayal which were in no way beneficial to my healing process. I did not desire depression. A triumphant life required more. To pursue healing, it was imperative that I exercise faith, change my thoughts and set forth action. Therefore, I began with asking more empowering questions where the answers would encourage, compel and hopefully guide me upon a path of restoration. One such question was, *what must I learn or do to be healed?*

My first action to what I perceived as catastrophic news, was to search for a naturopathic doctor who could provide a natural and nonsurgical solution. Some may even suggest that I was in denial! Nonetheless, after many doctors' visits, I eventually listened to my present truth, followed the guidance of my medical doctor's advice and did what I came to believe was necessary for me to move toward life anew. I made the critical decision which resulted in several surgeries on my breasts.

In the very beginning while at home recuperating, my now young woman daughter recognized that I was a bit melancholy and low in spirit. One bright sunny day as she bounced down the steps on her way to work, she bellowed, "Mommy, see God today!" I had not heard those encouraging words for many years. Immediately, my countenance changed and I began to smile. The seed which I had planted several years ago had taken root and had come back to bear timely good fruit in my life!

Those three words caused me to look within and toward the light of God. As I had taught her, I began to reflect upon what was still very good and healthy about my life. I was reminded that I am a believer and recognized that I had to choose my thoughts. I began to intentionally focus on a healing path to move from the experience of my diagnosis and the subsequent outcome of my surgical procedure. The sad and hopeless thoughts of being diagnosed with breast cancer began to dissipate as I replaced them with higher, more appreciative thinking. I began to be grateful for those changeless, beautiful and wonderful things that were anchored in my life. I also began to reflect on the intricate connection between my mind and body. I knew that a positive high vibration-thinking and a low-level thinking could not occupy the same space in my thoughts.

There is a scripture that reminds us to "choose whom we shall serve." So I chose to stand firm on my belief that this ever-present God was still on hand and as a result, I soon felt transformed by a great sense of peace and reassurance that everything was going to be fine and work out as it should. This change was a direct result of my former declaratory affirmation to my daughter to *"See God Today!"*

With this perception, I reflected back upon the conversation with my co-worker and began to believe her sharing as the gracious hand of an all-knowing God prompting me to respond to a critical and unknown condition. Her act of courage and vulnerability undeniably encouraged me to act on my own health quest which led me to the knowledge of my newly-discovered life situation in a very timely manner. *"Seeing God Today"* suggests hope, changes one's perspective and leads toward a demeanor of humble gratitude.

"To See God" also helps me to better value and respect the impermanence of life and to choose to live more fully, become more vulnerable, to let go if necessary, and love more freely. I realized that despite my diagnosis of cancer, life was still present and that the greater part of me was still very healthy. I realized that I was more than my breasts and I was more than cancer. My spirit was lifted and

I began to write again. In essence, I felt an amazing, vibrant shift within me and was determined to live victoriously!

The battle against cancer is a courageous and tough one. Beyond the required traditional methods of healing, there are numerous ways in which persons impacted by cancer can reduce stress, remove negative energy, and renew positive mindsets to enhance their quality of life. We can choose to enjoy the best of what is left in our lives and make the necessary adjustments according to our diverse circumstances.

When impacted by cancer, there will be challenging days ahead. Today, we have the power to look beyond our immediate circumstances to encounter the grace of God to sustain us. So give yourself permission to perceive what is still good in your life and give thanks. Life is still in us and with us. Be encouraged to stretch your eyes of faith as we share this journaling experience together.

As you begin to journal, reflect and write about where or how you did *see God today*.

Did You?

Have a good day?
Share a smile?
Sing out loud?
Give a hug?
See the sky?
Enjoy the weather?
Receive a kindness?
Get a compliment?
Do some exercise?
Laugh with friends?
Find a treasure?
Pay a bill?
Save a dollar?
Take a nap?
Enjoy a movie?
Feel some love?
Kiss the kids?
Turn on music?
Dance a little?
Read a book?
Shoot the breeze?
Smell the flower?
Taste the food?
Breathe the air?
Live the day?

Where did you *See God Today*?

At home or in your bedroom?

_____

_____

_____

_____

_____

_____

_____

_____

_____

_____

_____

_____

_____

_____

_____

_____

_____

_____

_____

_____

_____

_____

_____

_____

_____

_____

Listening to music?

Making a meal?

With nature?

Receiving or giving?

_____

_____

_____

_____

_____

_____

_____

_____

_____

_____

_____

_____

_____

_____

_____

_____

_____

_____

_____

_____

_____

_____

_____

_____

_____

_____

_____

_____

_____

_____

Gratitude

While driving along?

Through personal care?

_____

_____

_____

_____

_____

_____

_____

_____

_____

_____

_____

_____

_____

_____

_____

_____

_____

_____

_____

_____

_____

_____

_____

_____

_____

_____

_____

_____

Gratitude

Through prayer and meditation?

Meeting someone new?

_____

_____

_____

_____

_____

_____

_____

_____

_____

_____

_____

_____

_____

_____

_____

_____

_____

_____

_____

_____

_____

_____

_____

_____

_____

_____

_____

_____

Gratitude

Overcoming physical or emotional pain?

_____

_____

_____

_____

_____

_____

_____

_____

_____

_____

_____

_____

_____

_____

_____

_____

_____

_____

_____

_____

_____

_____

_____

_____

_____

_____

_____

Financial blessing?

Gratitude

In silence or being alone?

_____

_____

_____

_____

_____

_____

_____

_____

_____

_____

_____

_____

_____

_____

_____

_____

_____

_____

_____

_____

_____

_____

_____

_____

_____

_____

_____

Renewed strength/exercise?

Gratitude

Experiencing an act of kindness?

_____

_____

_____

_____

_____

_____

_____

_____

_____

_____

_____

_____

_____

_____

_____

_____

_____

_____

_____

_____

_____

_____

_____

_____

_____

_____

_____

Friends and family?

Gratitude

Reading a book?

_____
_____
_____
_____
_____
_____
_____
_____
_____
_____
_____
_____
_____
_____
_____
_____
_____
_____
_____
_____
_____
_____
_____
_____
_____

Enjoying your day?

Gratitude

Service or support to another?

_____

_____

_____

_____

_____

_____

_____

_____

_____

_____

_____

_____

_____

_____

_____

_____

_____

_____

_____

_____

_____

_____

_____

_____

_____

_____

_____

Doing something creative?

_____

_____

_____

_____

_____

_____

_____

_____

_____

_____

_____

_____

_____

_____

_____

_____

_____

_____

_____

_____

_____

_____

_____

_____

_____

_____

_____

_____

Gratitude

During the warmth of sunshine on a beautiful day?

Taking a short trip?

JOURNALING 2

Contemplations

*Whoever offers a sacrifice of thanksgiving glorifies me,
and I will reveal the salvation of God to
whomever continues in my way.*

— PSALM 50:23 (ISV)

My Gratitude Journal Entry

I give thanks today that my true self
Is made in the image of God's Spirit and Truth.
Much greater is the light within my total being
Than the small dark blemish within my body.
I am grateful to know that I am more than cancer.
Therefore I can choose to live triumphantly today![4]

---

[4] "You never know how strong you are until being strong is the only choice you have.", Bob Marley, Songwriter/Artist, https://psychology-spot.com/you-never-know-how-strong-you-are-until/

There was a leader whom I heard had encouraged a team of players by saying, *"It's not whether you get knocked down, it's whether you get up."* Life brings with it numerous and various challenges. Upon the journey of human experience, everyone will lose, stumble, or fall at some point in life. However, what makes the obvious difference between those who fall and those who rise is one simple action and that is....getting up.

For those of us desiring a better life experience, mutual love, and incredible joy, we must persevere and resist being stuck in a pitiful state of despair, defeat, and hopelessness. Change begins within us and requires action if we sincerely yearn to improve. Learning from our past and moving ahead, requires that we are brave and faithful enough to live as if there is more to life and that God has greater opportunities awaiting us. The Lord gently calls upon us to get up and get moving after we fall. Remember that the Bible says:

"For a righteous man falls seven times, and rises again..."
— *Proverbs 24:16 (NASB)*

My Gratitude Journal Entry

My gratitude journey today:

_____

_____

_____

_____

_____

_____

_____

_____

_____

_____

_____

_____

_____

_____

_____

_____

_____

_____

_____

_____

_____

_____

_____

_____

_____

_____

My Gratitude Journal Entry

*A*n actress once said that *"being grateful is like riches and complaining is like poverty"*. I have had days of dissatisfaction where I did not see anything working in my favor, feeling as if nothing was going right for me. That level of consciousness left me feeling needy, lacking and annoyed. As a result, it created an impoverished mindset which radiated a very low vibratory energy-field. Persistent grief and unrelenting complaint attracts more scarcity, hardship, and negativity. The lower I thought, the emptier and more disgraceful things appeared.

On the other hand, when expressing gratitude, we perceive beyond and above our circumstances. Gratitude refines our perspective, raises the energy level, radiates beauty, uplifts our countenance and opens a path of opportunity to experience more than what meets the eye. It redirects our thoughts and diverts us from the immediate or negative happenstance toward embracing appreciation and joy. This not only diminishes but overcomes the feeling of being in a state of lack. It restores our confidence that we still possess a quality of richness in our daily lives.

Gratitude will cause us to be present to the vast blessings we possess. You will find that being thankful will draw more joy and blessing toward you. Choose to see an abundant universe of good that is filled with life, joy and love because it is the will of our Heavenly Father toward us. Be reminded that the Bible teaches:

The Lord is My Shepherd. I shall not want.
—Psalm 23:1 (NASB)

My gratitude journey today:

_____

_____

_____

_____

_____

_____

_____

_____

_____

_____

_____

_____

_____

_____

_____

_____

_____

_____

_____

_____

_____

_____

_____

_____

_____

_____

_____

_____

_____

_____

_____

My Gratitude Journal Entry

My Gratitude Journal Entry

The Bible teaches us that: "Even though I walk through the valley of the shadow of death, I will fear no evil, for you are with me." (Psalms 23:4, ESV) Figuratively, a valley is a low and depressed space. Many will suffer a valley experience while on life's journey. According to the scripture, this particular valley is accompanied by the shadow of death.

What is important to consider is that death in this valley is only a shadow. It is not actual, firm or capable of stopping the power of God. The *shadow* of death is illusory and nebulous. Its existence indicates that light is near but it is blocked and encumbered. Therefore, when we find ourselves experiencing a dreadful sense of fear, remember that you are focusing on a space where the light is not. Look to the light!

Disempowering thoughts of fear, self-pity, and discouragement are the shadowy illusions that hinder the light of peace. Fear not and trust that the Light of God is with you even while in the lowest places in your life. Written in Psalms, King David declared his fearlessness because he believed in the presence of God as he walked through the valley of the shadow of death.

Give thanks because we are not yet at our end. Our eyes of faith will help us get through. God is still present even in our valley moments. This scripture should help to reassure you:

The Lord is near to all who call on him, to all who call on him in truth.
— *Psalm 145:18 (NIV)*

My Gratitude Journal Entry

My gratitude journey today:

_____

_____

_____

_____

_____

_____

_____

_____

_____

_____

_____

_____

_____

_____

_____

_____

_____

_____

_____

_____

_____

_____

_____

_____

_____

_____

_____

My Gratitude Journal Entry

It is important to *"Look at what you have not what you had and be grateful."*[5] After surgery, my body and my breasts, in particular, were forever changed. No longer did I have the large, voluptuous bosom that I was familiar with. Initially, I was not comfortable or happy with this smaller version of my body. Yet, the Holy Spirt of Truth reminded me that my identity is not in my body and that beauty is so much more.

I had to reevaluate my thoughts because I could not have a fulfilling life or combat my condition tied to or defined by the past. Yesterday was. Today is. I am grateful to be alive and for what has become my new reality. My past was a wonderful blessing but it no longer characterized me. Holding on to the past blinded me to the gift of my present and future. "Whatever my past experience, I may fall, remain, or rise according to my thoughts. I will become as small as my weakest idea or as great as my dominant aspiration."[6]

So I move forward embracing a new sense of my well-being and appreciation for the presence of beauty that life has still rewarded me. Being actively grateful helps me to remember that cancer could not rob me of my essential beauty, self-love, quiet strength, and perseverance that possess me. I am reminded and reinforced by the word of God which says:

I count not myself to have apprehended:
but this one thing I do, forgetting those things which are behind,
and reaching forth unto those things which are before,

— PHILIPPIANS 3:13 (KJV)

---

[5] Suze Orman, Author, financial advisor and motivational speaker
[6] James Allen, Author, As a Man Thinketh

My gratitude journey today:

_____

_____

_____

_____

_____

_____

_____

_____

_____

_____

_____

_____

_____

_____

_____

_____

_____

_____

_____

_____

_____

_____

_____

_____

_____

My Gratitude Journal Entry

My Gratitude Journal Entry

As a believer in Christ, I embrace the idea that there is a dimension within us that is secure, enduring, and unwavering. This firm stillness is available for us to access through prayer for strength, guidance, and calmness. It is a space beyond the control and influence of the world's definition of us, the doctor's diagnosis, or our current condition.

There are many stories of those whom have accessed this inner wisdom and healing power of God. This space of grace has often been characterized with being ordered and established by everlasting love and divine intelligence. Christ within is the expression of this "stainless beauty" and through Christ, I believe that I am connected to the unfailing principles of love, grace, power, healing, gentleness, forgiveness, clarity, and fearlessness.

Therefore, I am able to press forward undeterred by fear of the unknown and rise above hopelessness. In this strength, I can still love freely. I can still smile authentically. I can think intentionally and I can still have joy unspeakably because of this unchangeable realm within which is not controlled by my body or the circumstances of my flesh. It never leaves even if I choose to yield under the weight of disappointment. I have the option to choose again and when I make the decision to stand on this solid ground with gratitude, I open myself to the hope of attaining the strength and encouragement I need to live forward. The following scripture reinforces my belief as it states:

"Therefore, since we are receiving a kingdom that cannot be shaken;
let us be thankful, and so worship God acceptably
with reverence and awe."

—*HEBREW 12:28 (NIV)*

My Gratitude Journal Entry

My gratitude journey today:

_____

_____

_____

_____

_____

_____

_____

_____

_____

_____

_____

_____

_____

_____

_____

_____

_____

_____

_____

_____

_____

_____

_____

_____

_____

_____

_____

My Gratitude Journal Entry

Many of us have heard the expression, *"when we change our thoughts, we change our world."*[7] There are those who have written extensively on the idea that what occurs in the physical is often an outcome of our thoughts and a reflection of our mindsets. Therefore, when we think ourselves into depression, hopelessness, and self-pity, it causes us to feel sadness and discontent which impacts our relationships. This state of being does not provoke or inspire healing. If we desire to experience the strength of healing, including the love for self and others, we must guard our hearts by being attentive to what we allow to enter. May we always consider the atmosphere of our thoughts.

As we choose thoughts that express gratitude, we bring positivity to our environment which unlocks a door and clears the way for the probability of encountering incredible blessings. As believers, we are still the salt of the earth. Making the decision to change for the better begins with prayer, cutting edge thinking, and embracing a greater vision for our lives. This requires faith and work to bring this outcome into existence, as the Word of God encourages us to...

"Do not be conformed to the pattern of this world,
but be transformed by the renewing of your mind..."

—ROMANS 12:2 (NIV)

---

[7] Norman Vincent Peale, Minister and Author, Power of Positive Thinking, 1952

My gratitude journey today:

My Gratitude Journal Entry

My Gratitude Journal Entry

"We can never manifest a desirable physical state while entertaining an undesirable mental state."[8] There have been longtime conversations about the body-mind connection. During the time when my family life became impacted by separation, my daughter was very young and developed a heart condition which caused me to take her to the hospital. The doctors advised me that her heartbeats were broken, erratic, and skipping normal pace. They suggested that she undergo open-heart surgery. I was more than alarmed and prayed for guidance. Being quiet and confident in the providence of God, I developed an insight which prompted me to take another step before surrendering to surgery.

Her doctor stated that the beating pattern of my daughter's heart appeared to indicate that there could be a breakage in the heart valve and made plans to place her on a heart monitoring machine. Suddenly, a thought occurred to me and I began to contemplate whether this physical condition was a result of her painful thoughts about our family separation which could have actually broken her heart. Before the heart-monitoring machine was received, I began to speak healing, love, and gratitude over her life and took her to several prayer sessions for hope and healing.

Soon thereafter, while on my way home from work, a little lost puppy ran over to me. I picked it up, took it home, and gave it to my daughter. She was so grateful and happy. Over a period of time, I noticed that as joy sprung up from within her, she began to laugh out loud and play cheerfully again. I also recognized that she was not complaining about her rapid heartbeats. Her happiness and gratitude about her new puppy had a positively stunning impact.

Eventually, I took her back to the doctor for her scheduled appointment and surprisingly, there were no signs of erratic broken heart palpitations or a problematic heart condition! Today, it has been more than twenty years and she has not needed surgery and neither has there been any further heart problems. I would not suggest this

---

[8] Frederick Bailes, Author and Teacher

for anyone because I would have eventually taken her for surgery. Nonetheless, that experience confirmed that our thoughts and feelings can hinder or foster healing and with the power of prayer, gratitude and the Grace of God, we are overcomers. So I encourage you to:

"Be of good courage and He shall strengthen your heart,
all you that hope in the Lord."

— *PSALM 31:24 (NKJV)*

My gratitude journey today:

_____

_____

_____

_____

_____

_____

_____

_____

_____

_____

_____

_____

_____

_____

_____

_____

_____

_____

_____

_____

_____

_____

_____

_____

_____

_____

_____

_____

_____

My Gratitude Journal Entry

My Gratitude Journal Entry

"*There is no outer progress without inner change.*"[9] It would be so easy to simply lie in bed or sit by our window and wait for a positive change to come. However, when we want to see outward change, it begins with inner work. Here, we begin with taking action in our thought world because the atmosphere of our lives corresponds often with the quality of our thinking. Thoughts founded on the negative have poor consequences. Therefore, we will begin our healing breakthrough with a candid conversation in the mirror of self, observing and addressing the personal, secret thoughts we harbor and rehearse in our minds.

The familiar expression "as within, so without," reminds us that our outer world is a reflection of what is going on within our minds. If this is true, we must see our lives through a different lens if we sincerely desire and believe we can enjoy a greater life. Remember to let go of blaming others and ourselves. Forgive. Unfortunately, the past will not change but the good news is, we can! Meditate on Christ in a spirit of appreciation with words that inspire and uplift you. This inner work is the groundwork for favorable outer change and progressive forward movement.

As a result of this process, we will develop the inner structure and mental apparatus to live our faith and make the choices that move us in the direction of our greatest healing and personal empowerment. Remember:

Therefore we do not lose heart. Though outwardly we are wasting away, yet inwardly we are being renewed day by day.

—*2 CORINTHIANS 4:16 (NIV)*

---

[9] Joseph Murphy, Author and Minister

My Gratitude Journal Entry

My gratitude journey today:

My Gratitude Journal Entry

"*Spend your thoughts being happy about the future, not sad about the past.*"[10] Be grateful that cancer has not taken you away. You are still able to share, love, read, write, sing or create and bring beauty. Cancer may have impacted your journey and changed your life as did so many other things, but you must strive to live the best you can now!

Our future may be for a day, a month, or years. Everyone will have to let this journey go one day...but for today, you still have another opportunity to live, love, and share. You have endured the past diagnosis and the physical changes in your body and today, you will uncover a new joy. Although the quantity of your days are a mystery, you have the power to energize and influence the quality of your moments. Therefore, enjoy today and look forward to the next moment with hope and gratitude. Plan to live and *"See God"* along the way because:

> *"You keep him in perfect peace*
> *whose mind is stayed on you*
> *because he trusts in you."*
>
> —ISAIAH 26:3 (ESV)

---

[10] Suze Orman, Ibid.

My gratitude journey today:

_____

_____

_____

_____

_____

_____

_____

_____

_____

_____

_____

_____

_____

_____

_____

_____

_____

_____

_____

_____

_____

_____

_____

_____

_____

_____

_____

My Gratitude Journal Entry

My Gratitude Journal Entry

"*Your words have the power to create or the power to destroy. The choice is up to you.*"[11] We have a significant ability to affect our environment by the words we use. In Proverbs 18:21, the writer reminds us that, *"life and death are in the power of the tongue."* Such a powerful, creative tool! That is why it is so important to be conscientious of our thoughts which are the roots of our feelings. The words we use are the reflections of these feelings and more deeply, our beliefs.

We will reap from the thoughts we sow. With the power of words, we build ourselves up or hinder our healing process. "Good thoughts bear good fruit."[12] To *"See God Today"* is a legitimate and creative action. It encourages a mindset of gratitude, changes our language, and inspires us to see things in a different manner. We impact our lives with the words we choose and the Bible underscores it with this scripture:

*"What goes into someone's mouth does not defile them,
but what comes out of their mouth, that is what defiles them."*

—*MATTHEW 15:11 (NIV)*

---

[11] Suze Orman, Ibid.

[12] James Allen, As a Man Thinketh, pg 7

My Gratitude Journal Entry

My gratitude journey today:

My Gratitude Journal Entry

"*Focus on what you are moving toward rather than what you are leaving behind.*"[13] We may have cried yesterday because of what we thought we had lost, but we are reminded of the beautiful parts of our lives that still exist in spite of any physical changes, challenges and adjustments.

I was living a very productive and rewarding life and I intend to continue doing the same. Yesterday was a moment in time and a part of my beautiful story. Just as there were blessings then, there are blessings in my today as I plant seeds for tomorrow. I have come to appreciate the importance of releasing anxiety and letting go of worry especially over a past of which I have no control.

The clock is not moving backwards. Forgive yourself and release unnecessary thoughts that cause stress and dis-ease. We do not know how much longer we have to enjoy this experience called life. Let us exercise our will to keep moving onward with anticipation and hope for the greater possibilities before us.

We are made in the image of a benevolent and inexpressible Creator, therefore, we are endowed with an inordinate amount of creative power and potential working within us. I encourage you to breakthrough and advance with your thoughts set toward hope and a bright new day. Be encouraged and remember to:

"Forget the former things; do not dwell on the past.
See, I am doing a new thing!

—*Isaiah 43:18-19 (NIV)*

---

[13] Alan Cohen, Author

My gratitude journey today:

_____

_____

_____

_____

_____

_____

_____

_____

_____

_____

_____

_____

_____

_____

_____

_____

_____

_____

_____

_____

_____

_____

_____

_____

_____

_____

_____

_____

My Gratitude Journal Entry

My Gratitude Journal Entry

A happy person is not a person in a certain set of circumstances, but rather a person with a certain set of attitudes."[14] Some people may wonder if it is possible to experience joy when diagnosed with cancer because it is such a time of deep sorrow, disappointment, and fear. Anyone diagnosed with this disorder will feel pain and sadness while journeying through this exhausting and arduous experience, but it is possible to be comforted.

To *"See God Today"* will bring a moment of relief. It encourages those of us on this journey to reflect with a mindset of optimism regardless of our circumstances. It enables us to appreciate the effortless breath of life and see beyond the darkness of the diagnosis toward the light of hope. This is a magnificent grace that renders us the strength to move from here to there; from anxiety to assurance; and from hurt to healed.

While the critical occurrence of cancer will certainly impact the condition of our lives, our attending attitudes will affect the quality of our days. Attitude is a mindset. It is essentially the result of the way we feel, think, and respond to the various things that happen to us. If our desire is to find authentic joy or a greater measure of contentment during turbulent seasons in our lives, we must be deliberate in our thoughts and intentionally take action without apology or excuse. Blessedness and happiness does not begin with material possessions but with our thoughts.

Circumstances may change, but we are more than the situations in our lives. I encourage you to set your thoughts upon a vision that would allow your energy to rise above the storm much like the splendid flight of the fearless eagle. I cannot emphasize enough how our feelings reflect our thoughts and how being appreciative of our amazing journey in Christ is the key to experiencing happiness. When we elevate our thoughts, God grants us the probable outcome and favor to have a positive impact on our lives. Below is a clear reminder from the Bible which says:

---

[14] Hugh Downs, Retired American Broadcaster, TV Host, Author

"Whatsoever things are true, whatsoever things are honest, whatsoever things are just, whatsoever things are pure, whatsoever things are lovely, whatsoever things are of good report; there be any virtue and if there be any praise, think on those things."

—PHILIPPIANS *4:8 (KJV)*

My gratitude journey today:

_____

_____

_____

_____

_____

_____

_____

_____

_____

_____

_____

_____

_____

_____

_____

_____

_____

_____

_____

_____

_____

_____

_____

_____

_____

_____

_____

_____

My Gratitude Journal Entry

My Gratitude Journal Entry

"*Each moment in life is magical, precious and will never exist again.*"[15] At the rising of sun, I am able to open my eyes again. Thank you! I inhale deeply and again experience the breath of life. Thank you! I realize that this brand new, untouched, fresh morning I will never see again and this day, I have never experienced before. In this new morning, there are no negatives (except in my memory/thought). This moment brings brand new mercies and an open fresh canvas for me to pilgrimage, paint, and express my creative ingenuity. I choose this day!

Each moment of today brings with it new opportunities to be grateful. So I ask myself, what can I do to make this day richer? I can begin with "*Seeing God!*" I can begin with gratitude. "Thank you Jesus!" Being grateful for life's precious moments will bring more light on the journey expanding our path of wellness. So let us fully experience that...

> "*...Morning by morning He wakens me*
> *and opens my understanding to his will.*"
>
> —ISAIAH 50:4 (NLT)

---

[15] Susan Taylor, Author, Editor and Writer

My Gratitude Journal Entry

My gratitude journey today:

_____

_____

_____

_____

_____

_____

_____

_____

_____

_____

_____

_____

_____

_____

_____

_____

_____

_____

_____

_____

_____

_____

_____

_____

_____

_____

My Gratitude Journal Entry

As I pressed forward, I heard a speaker say that *"the human Spirit is stronger than anything that can happen to it."*[16] This caused me to recall a time when I was a little girl and I went to visit my great aunt in the hospital who was dying from cancer. The memory that made the most everlasting impact was seeing how her body had become so small, weak, and frail, unlike the woman I knew before cancer. Yet, at the same time, her mind seemed very agile.

Her eyes were large and piercing as she looked at me with love and spoke to me with a kind, firm, and compelling voice. I do not recall all that she said but I remember the feeling of being perplexed in my understanding of death. I could not fathom how it were possible for her to look so gaunt and fragile while sounding like the strong, loving woman I knew.

For years, I was gripped by that memory. It was not until years later when I became aware of the amazing physical and metaphysical dimensions of the human being that I received understanding. In my younger years, I did not have insight of our spiritual quality or that my aunt was more than a physical body. However, that experience taught me that, without her consent, cancer could not overpower her love and gift as aunt to me. There was something deeper and more alive within her. Although cancer had physical leverage, it did not diminish the character of the woman I knew her to be.

Cancer is limited to the physical dynamics of our human anatomy. As a believer in Jesus Christ, I have come to know that there is a dimension of our lives that is alive, dynamic, creative and much stronger than anything that could happen to it. Although my aunt left this earth realm physically, the memory of her inner strength, the love she revealed, and the acquaintance with the greater life within still speak and lives with me today. For that I am truly grateful and can say:

> *"Thanks be to God for His inexpressible gift!"*
> —2 CORINTHIANS 9:15 (ESV)

---

[16] CC Scott, Poet

My gratitude journey today:

_____

_____

_____

_____

_____

_____

_____

_____

_____

_____

_____

_____

_____

_____

_____

_____

_____

_____

_____

_____

_____

_____

_____

_____

_____

_____

_____

My Gratitude Journal Entry

My Gratitude Journal Entry

"*We magnetize into our lives whatever we hold in our thoughts.*"[17] To magnetize is "to make larger, to lure, or to attract". There have been times when I have started my day with low-thought vibrations which caused me to feel sad and despondent. As a result, my day progressed with fatigue and heavy burden causing me to become easily irritated, frustrated, and tired. This negative thinking is non-productive. If I desired positive experiences, I had to discontinue low-level thinking.

I am confident that I possess the power to select my thoughts. Acting negatively indicates that I am having weak and unfavorable thoughts which causes me to radiate and attract more negativity bringing about that which does not uplift but distresses and troubles me. That thought process is a vicious cycle.

When I *See God*, my "territory is enlarged"[18] and I see beyond my situation. I am cognizant of the ever-present moments of joy and beauty in life. I also become a magnetic energy field for that which could enrich my well-being and energize my body. As a consequence, I feel better, give greater, and love more completely. I am reinforced by the word:

"Come near to God and he will come near to you."

—James 4:8 (NIV)

---

[17] Richard Bach, Author
[18] Bruce Wilkerson, Author, Prayer of Jabez, 2000

My Gratitude Journal Entry

My gratitude journey today:

My Gratitude Journal Entry

"*Peace does not mean to be in a place where there is no trouble, noise, or hard work. It means to be in the midst of such things and still find calm in your heart.*"[19] Gratitude is a tool that helps us to experience rest even while going through difficult times. It takes our mind off of our troubles and interrupts the darkness of pain with a moment of light. I believe this a significant part of the healing process.

As I was pressing forward upon the path of good health, creativity, and progressive contribution, I stumbled across my unsuspecting doctor's report of breast cancer. For a little while, I was immobilized by thoughts of disbelief and the fear of death. As a result, I was weakened in the ability to express the beauty of joy and peace that once strengthened me. I felt overwhelmed until I remembered my declaratory statement "See God Today." This compelled me to emotionally and thoughtfully disconnect from a burdensome fear and recognize God's present blessings.

Therefore, in the face of my new-found physical condition, I began to be thankful for other things in my life. "As the physically weak can make oneself strong by determined and consistent training, so the one of weak thoughts can increase strength by exercising the mind in gratitude and positive thinking."[20] So I took on the challenge to acknowledge my gifts and to do the hard work of healing that was before me. Jesus was able to calm the storm and say "Peace be still." I reminded myself that within me resides this power where the winds in my life surrender to my inner confidence in God. In this space, I began to encounter peace in the midst of my storm. So, I encourage you:

"*Do not be anxious about anything, but in every situation, by prayer and petition, with thanksgiving, present your requests to God. And the peace of God, which transcends all understanding, will guard your hearts and your minds in Christ Jesus.*
— PHILIPPIANS 4:6-7 (NIV)"

---

[19] Unknown
[20] James Allen, As a Man Thinketh

My gratitude journey today:

My Gratitude Journal Entry

My Gratitude Journal Entry

"*Healing occurs as you allow the Spirit of love to flow within you.*"[21] Sometimes, I see love as a gentle and blissful communion; an intercourse of healing and hope; a harmonious creative movement toward boundless peace, joy, and possibility. When the Holy Spirit of God moves through me, I am in unity with myself and others. Yet, I am reminded by poet, Khalil Gibran, that love may also grind, mold, trouble, prune, and bring burden for the purpose of moving us forward toward growth and a better version of ourselves.

In every sense, the power of love requires our permission to operate freely in our lives to do the inner work necessary to stimulate healing. Irritation and grief dwindles as we embrace ourselves with Godly patience, love and acceptance. In Christ, we are strengthened to launch forward taking the steps necessary to heal the mind, body and soul.

Be thankful. Encourage yourself. Pray through and know that love is powerful, intelligent, designed, and purposed to assist your healing journey. Never forget that the Word of God declares:

"Love never fails..."

—*1 Corinthians 13:8 (NIV)*

---

[21] Susan Taylor, Ibid.

My Gratitude Journal Entry

My gratitude journey today:

My Gratitude Journal Entry

"*We have the power and the responsibility to create peace and happiness in our lives and to ease the suffering in our world.*"[22] Although we may not feel up to it or may feel a little selfish at times, our lives are not our own. We are a part of a larger community. The gift of life is given to share and connect with others.

One smile can change the broken countenance of a longing heart or a desperate soul. Because of our divine design, a sense of fulfillment occurs when we share our gifts to help others within our social network. When I "*See God,*" I experience life beyond the boundaries of my own personal physical reality because God is so much more than one person. I also recognize that I am a part of the divine continuum of life connected to generations past and to come. I am a part of history.

Life did not begin with me and will not end with me. At the same time, "I am the end product of thousands of years of human development, therefore, I am equipped in both mind and body"[23] to press forward so that I may accomplish great things. All of us stand on the strong shoulders of a great history and our loved ones will stand on ours. Our story is but a page in a larger book of life and in Christ, we have a purpose to fulfill . I have discovered the richness of peace, pearls of love, and the jewels of wisdom through gratitude. This wealth is a part of my legacy.

My hope is restored and my life is greatly blessed as I share these nuggets of inspiration and encouragement to ease pain and to support others. I know that "*the God of all does comfort us in our troubles*" (2 Corinthians 1:3-4). It is his intention that we share the abundant life with those in need because:

> "*God is not unjust; he will not forget your work*
> *and the love you have shown him as*
> *you have helped his people and continue to help them.*"
> —*HEBREWS 6:10 (NIV)*

---

[22] Susan Taylor, Ibid.
[23] Og Mandino, Author, Greatest Salesman In The World

My gratitude journey today:

My Gratitude Journal Entry

My Gratitude Journal Entry

"*It is good to have an end to journey toward; but it is the journey that matters in the end.*"[24] I love to read a good book and every good book has an ending when the story is over. When there are no more chapters and nothing else to read, what remains is the impact left upon those who have read and experienced the pages written. From the beginning until the end, our pages of life will disclose a story that reveals the footsteps of our unique and interesting paths. This is where love happens, where suffering is encountered, where wisdom is developed, and where joy is discovered. With God, we have the ability to create a masterpiece.

"*Seeing God*" helps us to journey through the pages of our story with gratitude so that our memoir might witness the victory of living in Christ and be a testament of hope and blessing to others. When we "*See God,*" we realize that we are not defined by one moment, one experience, one failure or one success. Our story is greater than one chapter and the fullness of who we are has not yet appeared. We were born to discover the wisdom of living this life and not born to simply die. We have been granted this privilege to be actively engaged and to be the best we can be. We desire to experience life vibrantly, to give generously, to create newness and to appreciate our opportunity to be here.

God has provided us with a duration of time. We shall commit to that which would, by faith, catapult and guide us toward fulfillment. We will not be distracted with worry or burdened about our perceived misfortunes, but we will make this day the best day. When we reach the bank of the river where God grants us the blessed privilege to write the last page of our story, we will write it with the peace of knowing that we pursued what we believed to be true in Christ and fulfilled our purpose well. It takes courage, faith and action. May it be said at the end of our last chapter that:

---

[24] Ursula Kroeber Le Guin, Novelist

"We have fought the good fight, we have finished the race,
And we have kept the faith."

—2 TIMOTHY 4:7 (NIV)

My gratitude journey today:

My Gratitude Journal Entry

My Gratitude Journal Entry

"*In three words I can sum up everything I've learned about life: it goes on.*"[25] A great judge said to me that when her mother died, she wished that the world would pause for a moment while she suffered in mourning, but life events continued to proceed. Later when my mother died, I understood her sentiments. Her death caused me to stop in a season of sorrow as the world continued to unfold in spite of my loss. Life just kept moving. When cancer visited my body, time continued to move onward. It did not wait for me to catch up or get it together. The clock kept ticking. So, I had to make a decision.

I could have languished in pain or elect to trust God with my future. Settling in sadness and feelings of loneliness will keep one stuck in a time and frustrated with life. Lingering in hurt will not compel you to reach out and discover the hidden treasures planted in your today. Life goes on.

Gratitude encourages a sense of resiliency and opens the door of possibility. "Seeing God" helped me to set my sights higher and to get back into the race of life with intention, and to seek to rediscover my purpose. I am constantly encouraged by the following scripture and I hope you will be the same:

"For I know the plans I have for you, declares the LORD, plans to prosper you and not to harm you, plans to give you hope and a future."

—*JEREMIAH 29:11 (NIV)*

---

[25] Robert Frost, Poet

My Gratitude Journal Entry

My gratitude journey today:

My Gratitude Journal Entry

Afterword

" *Go out there and catch some magic.*"[26] The drama of life brings with it immense changes and immeasurable challenges but it is also full of grace, possibility and fascination. It is up to us to choose how we will perceive our experience and whether we will pursue the pathway of faith and gratitude where we might discover the amazing. Reach for it. Join a community of like-minded believers, connect with positive people, be kind, create beauty, pray, love and encourage one another. Life is here for us to love her, embrace her, and discover her wonders. Enjoy spending time with her to the best of your ability. There is so much we have to be thankful for. Give the power of gratitude the opportunity to comfort you. Have eyes to *"See God"* and remember:

> *Do not fear, for God is with you; do not be dismayed,*
> *for He is your God. He will strengthen you*
> *and help you; He will hold you up*
> *with His righteous right hand."*
>
> —Isaiah 41:10 (NIV)

The following is a brief exercise to invigorate your morning and for you to begin your day in a space of grace and gratitude. Please try it.

---

[26] Suze Orman, Ibid.

AWAKE UP, MY GLORY....

—*PSALM 57:8 (KJV)*

Glance into the mirror. Look deep within your eyes
And you will See God Today who deep within you lies.

Morning Mirror Exercise

- Stand/Sit in front of a facial mirror.
- Do not look at your facial features.
- Focus ONLY into the center of your eyes.
  "The eyes are the window of the soul."
- Take a very deep breath.
- Inhale and exhale slowly.
- Do not look left or right but directly into the center of your eyes.
- Call forward your inner strength and gifts.

SPEAK ALOUD the following:
- Good Morning God!
- Good Morning Life!
- Good Morning Health!
- Good Morning Strength!
- Good Morning Peace!
- Good Morning Wisdom!
- Good Morning Beauty!
- Good Morning Jesus!
- Good Morning _____(You fill in the blank!)

WAKE UP MY GLORY!
RISE, SHINE and WALK with me today
Thank you! Thank you! Thank you!

Conclusion

Thank you for this opportunity to co-journal with you celebrating together what is still wonderful in our lives.

As you meditate on the jewels of encouragement in this book, make your unique circumstances more meaningful by writing down the various ways you appreciate your gift of life. It is my hope and fervent prayer that this journal will inspire your faith, help you through your healing process, encourage joy and propel you toward an excellent mindset. While life is a quick dash between birth and death, we still have time to make it count! The quality of your life can be significantly improved when you exercise your faith and do the work.

Trust that the light of hope is still present! This creative journal is only to remind you of what you deeply know and that is, we are much more than cancer! With faith, we are confident that the Spirit of God is in and around us every day. By the power of the Holy Spirit, the proclamation "See God Today" brings us back to remembrance by announcing to our consciousness that life, love and beauty are still present. When our eyes are full of this light, radiance enters our body temples, bringing rest to our hearts, peace to our souls, and strength to our bodies. Our thirst is then quenched. I believe that this is a measure of healing.

Keep Journaling,
Choose Happiness,
Celebrate Life,
Pursue Peace.
And Be Well!
May God Bless and Keep You,
Amen

"Rejoice always,
Pray continually,
Give thanks in all circumstances;
For this is God's will for you in Christ Jesus."

—*1 Thessalonians 5:16-18 (NIV)*

References and Citations

THE AMERICAN BIBLE (KJV/NIV/ISV/NASB/NKJV/ESV/NLT)

RICHARD BACH

FREDERICK BAILES

MELODY BEATTIE

ALAN COHEN

DORIS DAY

JAMES ALLEN

OG MANDINO

HUGH DOWNS

ROBERT FROST

URSULA KROEBER LE GUIN

NORMAN VINCENT PEALE

JOSEPH MURPHY

BRUCE WILKERSON

BOB MARLEY

SUZE ORMAN

SUSAN TAYLOR

KHALIL GIBRAN

Back of Book

Although we share the same last name, the author has no family relation. "See God Today" is a priceless journal of gratitude. It reminds us that happiness is found in those moments when we are open to see and enjoy the blessings that God has to offer even in the midst of pain. Although it is written for those who are impacted by the experience of cancer, this book is able to minister to all who want to encounter life fully and fearlessly. It addresses life's issues in a very profound way and more importantly, it reminds us of the possibilities available through Christ who strengthens us. The author genuinely personifies the grace, passion and peace of gratitude through Jesus Christ, our Lord.

—Allison Lewis, LCSWC

About the Author

Linda Lewis is known as Faraja to many. As a cancer survivor, she seeks to creatively encourage others to practice self-healing and positive self-talk. As a passionate inspirational speaker and visionary Christian writer, she believes that the path of joy is accessible to those who earnestly pursue it with gratitude, faith and unwavering resilience. She has hosted women's empowerment sessions, held youth talks and is author of "Sister Songs", a book of prose and poetry.

Faraja has served as a national public speaker, has been awarded as a Champion of Courage by Fox 45, served several years as a radio talk show hostess of the Sister Circle on WEAA, 88.9 FM, holds a Master's Degree in Legal/Ethical Studies and is listed in Marquis Who's Who in the East. She works as an administrator for the state of Maryland and invites you to contact her at

FarajaNetwork@gmail.com
or
PO Box 4521
Baltimore, Maryland 21212

CPSIA information can be obtained at www.ICGtesting.com
Printed in the USA
BVHW040619030619
549979BV00006B/39/P

9 781640 882072